ON THE WATERBED THEY SANK TO THEIR OWN LEVELS

On the Waterbed They Sank to Their Own Levels

Sarah Rosenblatt

Drawings by Suzanne Rosenblatt

Carnegie Mellon University Press

Pittsburgh 2000

ACKNOWLEDGMENTS

The author expresses her gratitude to the editors of the following magazines and anthologies in which these poems first appeared: "Blindspot" in *The Brooklyn Review 3*, "The Man Without His Umbilical Chord" in *The Brooklyn Review 4*, "Hazardous Driving" in *The Haight-Ashbury Literary Review*, "Visiting New York" in *Heartland*, "Mom and Dad Growing Old" and "My Ex" in *Lucid Moon*, "Should I Stay or Should I Go?" and "Past Closing Time" in *Ploughshares*, "Yo-Yo" in *Poetry East*, "Leaving Home" in *The Portland Review*, and "Order" in the *Wildfire Anthology*. "Leaving Home," "Visiting New York," "Should I Stay or Should I Go?," "The Second Half of Our Lives," "The Procession," and "Mom and Dad Growing Old" were published in *American Poetry: The Next Generation*, edited by Gerald Costanzo and Jim Daniels.

I would like to thank my mother for her beautiful drawings and Laure Leplae-Arthur for all the help with the layout of the book. I would also like to thank Gerald Costanzo, without whom this book would not have been possible.

Publication of this book is supported by a grant from the Pennsylvania Council on the Arts.

Library of Congress Catalog Card Number 99-74770
ISBN 0-88748-331-3 Pbk.

Printed and bound in the United States of America
10 9 8 7 6 5 4 3 2 1

CONTENTS

For my parents and Craig and Cal.

A CERTAIN KIND OF LOVE

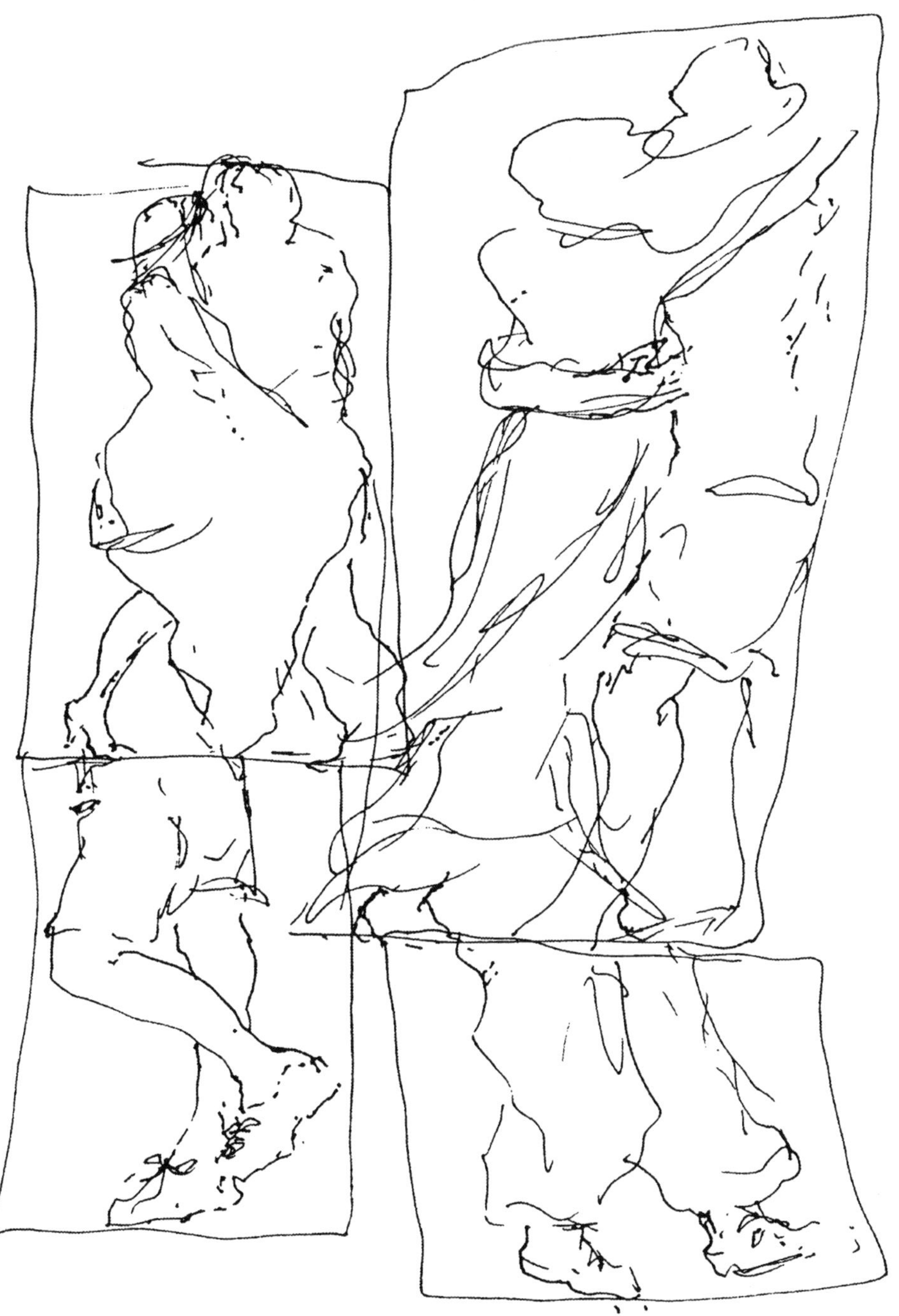

HAZARDOUS DRIVING

The road veered so far to the left,
we lost our right sides
when we rounded the corner.

We picked them up on our way back,
but always remembered what it was like
to be without...

except for the times when the moon
tumbled in the window, landed on the bed
and we fell into it.

PAST CLOSING TIME

We tore into each other's fragrances
enough to hold Wednesday
to its last possible moment,
but it swept across the windows
nevertheless.

He always set the table
and never cleared it,
hoping dinner would break through
into something that wouldn't wipe away.

They said it was past closing time at the Indian restaurant.
We both agreed it was still early,
even as they ushered us out the door.

THE MAN WITHOUT HIS UMBILICAL CHORD

The man without his umbilical chord—
nothing pulling him back
to the space between skyscrapers.

He was alone,
throttled by his speech,
atonal, like his ancestors,
alone, in his hooded coat.

It would take too much
to get in there.

I visited him recently—a kink in my forehead.
I could no longer sit on seats after he'd left them
and feel warmed.
I could only sit, dumbstruck, on his couch
with my aura in a paper bag.

THE CUSTODIAN

There was a tenderness
in the custodian's hands
that pulled at women,
but he never guessed.

Although he wasn't charged with his name,
he rode it through.

The space between his shoulders
carried more than it should.

The wind slurred his footprints
into those of a neighbor.

She smiled, letting sunshine in on her teeth
and between them.

The elastic in his socks
sunk in.

He knew how to carry the weather
and that sadness was
the distance between people.

LOSING THE SEASON

So many relaxed lunches
had reflected in their teeth
and blurred together.
Now, not one could pick itself out.

The child's cries
leave imprints in his mother's chewing gum.
She is only half aware of his prism eyes
and the dog exploring the puddle.

Spring came on gradually
like her husband's mustache.
When it finally crossed
his lip,
she couldn't remember.

GOOD MORNING THIS MORNING

She was tanned through
her lace leggings.
When she took them off,
he said she was calico.

The daylight came through
the curtains,
speckling their hug.

The dog slid
across the floor
and his reflection slid with him.

Love cascaded down her back
where only yesterday
had been ambivalence.

Was this something
she would hold to?

Or was it some kind
of rapidly depleting energy
that would get knocked

around
by her internal workings
and would have nothing
to do

with how she had said
good morning this morning?

THIRSTED FOR

Love was powdered out and thirsted for
by the window washer
as doorbells grew louder
than music on a Chinese train
and the doorman blew musk off his shoulder
into the wind.

From outside their bedroom
they sounded like paper accordions
pushing air in and out.
A cat's eye shone through the keyhole
leaving light on the wall
in which the shadows of two people
were folding and unfolding.

No way of knowing just how far the affair would go
as the cosmic reticulum boomed into the shades.
They kept them down
so the sun wouldn't come in
in the morning
and beat into their teeth.

WHAT DEVELOPS

In the darkroom her look came undone,
floating in the fluid.
He tried to connect it,
but it evaded his touch.

Although he was filled with kindness,
his name didn't break
the tension
in her face.

In the bathtub
love puckered on his fingers.
Each one was her
in a different state.
He stayed in the water.

Her eyes slid across
his name
and stopped before the last two letters.
She couldn't read him.
And she was always a foot behind
her kindness.

His boyhood
buried in his pillow
left patterns on his cheeks
that helped push sadness
further into the future.

Looking at the aboriginal expressions
in his childhood pictures,
he was dripping with changes
he'd been through.
No one licked them off.
They were all his.

ON THE WATERBED THEY SANK TO THEIR OWN LEVELS

Matters that had never been resolved
wrinkle on her eyelid
like lines on a prayer plant leaf.
These will never transfer to her lover.
They are hers to roll with.

And his events are scattered across
his partly opened eyes—
a man whose sleep is filled
with flinches.

Reading had let them know more
of who they were
and sleep blended it all together,
so the knowing became unknown
and appeared under their faces
at moments.

Hindsight

LEAVING HOME

The 5:30 light fell onto the dining room table,
pushed through the juice in our glasses
and slid bright orange along our forks.

We talked and laughed at dinner,
losing our faces in mouthfuls.

Later, my mother curled up in the purple chair;
my father lugged his laundry up the stairs;
and I remembered I was waiting for a train.

Our faces fell to their borders
like cakes in the oven
when someone has jumped.

HINDSIGHT

She sat on her glasses, crushed them,
and squinted into her past.
She swallowed—and could it be her mother's
esophagus the spaghetti was sliding down?

She had an indeterminate amount of luggage
and too few days to throw into it.
The time to leave was coming too near
like the face on the other side
of the window
carrying glimpses of her into the marshes
and lost fields.
The day fell.

Artichoke hearts went kaput
beneath their leaves.

And she woke up at the age of 22 with a past
and moved with it, though she didn't understand
the way it broke through to her face.

The blue sky falls on the brown table
and turns purple.
The man sleeping on the table
has turned pink.
She doesn't know what color she has become.
A bald man looks up;
the back of his head wrinkles into a baby's face.

YO-YO

The bright orange yo-yo whizzes,
yellow light whipping down its sides.
It reflects his mother on the right
his father on its left,
whirls them together.

“That's a repulsive way of saying that.”
“You are repulsive.”
And the word repulsive sinks
to the bottom of the boy
and he pushes it up
and down,
faster and faster.

IN MEMORY OF MY DOG, LILAC

Sleep was all over
the house.

Each of us took a couch.

The dog curled in all
the breathing.

She had an understanding of each
of us
through our breaths.

She knew us
through and through.

We had spent
so many afternoons this way.

VISITING NEW YORK

It's a wandering kind of crazy way I'm taken
out of one place I always am and put into another place
I rarely am. And rare faces stare at me in rare spaces.
And eyes wander over the surface of my skin and then land
on the billboard or band playing behind me. And it's behind me
the eyes linger as I linger within,
gasping at the emphasis placed on other things.
But nothing emphasized here is emphasized there.
And emphasis is a matter of extremes
that evens out. And the street cleaner drives by
and the light from the pink and blue sign hits
the white table and runs along its surface
until it hits bigger and better things.

LEAVING

The absence of flesh was too much to bear,
so I barely caught the train.
You don't expect to hear the tearing of leaves,
castration, or anything that leaves you divided.
It's a relief to see old friends, to realize
you're a definite pattern in someone's head.
The Rockefeller Center is floating away
as they take my picture and I watch passers-by
at convenient angles.
Levels of hope fall from my forehead as pokerfaced men
retrieve their dogs and crawl off into alleys.

MOURNINGS

I wake up and my stomach wants to walk away.
Homesickness like seasickness—
you're on a boat and you want to get off.
Struggling through this everyday hair,
I know there's time to use my fingers as matches
and burn off my friends; one
by one the days grow easier.
It's just the dull knocking at the window
that's disruptive to my health.

Healthy people walk through streets and hold their pockets.

And moving through a field, discovering the unorthodox
behavior of ants is as disconcerting as stretching
my body over a rock and feeling an incessant itch.
There is no itch that drives me on but the future
of shoes that will tie every morning
and shirts that will button.

SUNDAY EVENING

There's something slow and damaging
about Sunday evening.
It's not possible to redistribute
already distributed weight.
Just as it's not possible to get back stability
in an area prone to earthquakes.
Thinking about those I miss and used to see
at lunch and supper,
I take a nap in the early evening.
Waking, I'm shocked with being,
like a toe caught in a beer can.

FOURTH-FLOOR YOUNG ADULTS

Four anorexics play Scrabble,
the word "idea"
in the middle.
It's six o'clock.
The walls are knit yellow,
the carpet coral.

Mary Rose is lying on the green couch
reading *If You Really Knew Me, Would You Like Me?*

And Wanda in light purple is watching
an old man on TV talk about chocolate
pecan cookies.

Emaciated Kim slowly chews
on an apple which is
bitten into the shape of her face.

May looks like a cover girl,
but thinks she's homely.
She told her husband to pack the gun
when they moved,
so she could shoot herself
by the lake.
She's worried about her children,
the way she's raising them,
repeating her mother's recipes.

Emmy whimpers because she whimpers
and says she'll never like herself.

And Carolina holds anger
at her abusive father
tight into the corners of her face.

Louise, the woman with a man living inside her,
lights up a cigarette.

TEN YEAR HIGH SCHOOL REUNION

Her voice ruled, undid the air.
She'd been mean when she was young.
Now only a tidbit of that showed through
on her eyelid,
a sty,
that would no longer put you down,
would only throw you
when you looked at her on the level.

DECORATING THEIR OWN INTERIORS

DECORATING THEIR OWN INTERIORS

She thinks of herself as a sex object
but others think she's purely intelligent.

He is still in bed,
stuck in the warm indent
he's made for himself.

The neighbors glide by.
The wind makes them nervous
but also lets them know where they are.
Their hair upright on their heads;
their laughter bordering on their senses.

She was loving
but it was only a certain kind of loving,
shook up by nervousness.
He took it for what it was
and gave back
his splash-dash kind of kindness
in a push-me pull-you way.

BREAKING OUT

She was breaking out of her clothing.
Her body wanted to say one more thing
that her voice couldn't.

He was practical
and ran his hand
over the impracticality in her hair,
let it slide into his lifeline.

At least soon they'd get rid of their waterbed,
no longer leave their imprints deep
in a bed that would lose them
as soon as they stood up.

And it had been disconcerting
to sink so far back into an amniotic state
and wake to an adult mindset.

PROGRESSION

Or maybe I was only imagining the love;
and his face, with all its unsettling expressions,
could only settle into lust.

It was strange when he pulled the rug
out from under my laughter,
tugged like a lonely boy
in the middle of *Paradise Lost.*
I wanted him, but he was back at the ranch.

A new man came, a warmer one, less sewn
into his jacket—
more his name
than word of mouth.
He seemed to stand on his own,
though I could barely see him
as I watched myself in his mirrored glasses
explaining my shelves.

SHOULD I STAY OR SHOULD I GO?

I wonder where it is we belong
when daybreak wrinkles your new coat,
and pleasant is a word that rhymes with buckle.
I've been more or less unbuckling
into the late afternoon.
I've been hurt by your excursions,
not knowing the Chinese word for *go.*
There are stuffed animals with words written
along their bodies, torn and desiccating in the closet.
And men whose microphones reach further
into the afternoon than my shoes.

INSTRUMENT OF FLIGHT

Love sunk under her fingernails
bits that could never be dug out,
that ached when things went wrong.

Kindness was in his mouth
but could it extend
through his arms
to his hands?

Sex took over
and she became his instrument
of flight
to his other world.
She might as well have been faceless.

CRUSH

You aren't thinking about me
as I talk about China and the men who carried us
on rickshaws through the dark streets.
You're watching my teeth
that remind you of your mother's.

You make it difficult,
naked, in the middle of the room,
drawing pastel drawings of women
throwing noise at men.

It can't mean nothing that you write poems about women
who turn into monsters and take up more
than their share of the bed.
But you have left your underwear in my shoes.

ON THE FAR SHORE (after Tiananmen Square)

Most of the Chinese at the university are married.
They have an easier time
choosing who will be with whom.

And their faces are settled, rested—
like the face of someone floating
on his back

in tune with the water behind him and the sky in front of him
that drops to his wet belly
and jiggles along its smoothness.

Life is easier when you have someone
waiting for you at the far shore.

They come, coupled, to the library reading room,
read about
their families.

They read
and cringe, together.

The sun
a dark
cloud

BEHIND THEIR WINDOW

They were finding it difficult to unwind.
Nothing centered their misfortune
in a place where they could swallow.

And the man disrobing thought nothing
of his body.

And the woman watching
believed him.

A woman on the outside
knew better

and she let him know

even though his toes showed
through his shoes,
telling her the weather he had been through.

TAKEN CARE OF

The gutters push her family's essence
around the perimeters of their house,
telling the neighborhood who they are.

Her father used to read to her.
Now he's too busy.
She'll have to take the stories in
on her own.

She made it through high school,
pressed ahead into her college years
which broke open,
gave her bulk reason.

It helped to have a lover.
He took care of her carelessness.
She took care of his precision.
They measured each other
with their parents' hands.

IT WON'T WORK

All things indefinable exist in sequence
around my waist, orbiting the walls
and my shoes.

And the patterns that define themselves
in your hair
are patterns I want to touch.

As the leaves gather between us
the wind blows and you kick them with your bare feet
and tell me it's more difficult than you had imagined—
and imagining isn't enough.

But *enough* is the small eyelid that covers the eye,
And the twitch that slips beneath the lid
and beats to the person beneath
beats alone
unattended

by our conversation
that moves in and out of your hair,
changing positions in the wind.

THE WAY THE STORY WENT

The night watchman
was breathing into the windows,
and the forest fires were expanding
off the left bank
as the Chinese wrote their language
all over the walls,
pounding my color
into the night watchman's hair and
he isn't divisible by two
and he's only part of his chew.
He's only partly going to listen,
drinking in his inference.
And sadness was tucked into my neck.

THEY

The husband was as self-involved as the wife.
This made things easier, since neither
felt guilty for perusing the depths
of who they were
without coming up for air.

She was a martyr to a cause engrained in her forehead.

He left a deeper indentation in the bed
than she.
Did this mean he took things more to heart?

She was as sweet as can be
although the core of her nature was absorbed.
Her pleading with him to put down his sadness
was skin deep,
taking away her true voice
like a microphone.

BLINDSPOT

The light diagonally cuts across the elderly couple
in the beige car.
Their poodle hangs out the window,
its ears blowing back in the wind.

The couple's white hairs match their poodle's;
the dog's mouth is open, glinting sunlight
off its teeth.

And I remembered my blindspot.
When my dog died, I couldn't feel.
I let the glint of his teeth, reflected in my eyes,
bounce off.

And now maybe I can understand you
who shake off your whole childhood
like a dog shaking off water.

Maybe I can understand...
but if you had a dog and a car,
you'd close all the windows
and cover them with dark paper.

A FAMILY OF INDIVIDUALS

He said, "I married you
because you come from a family of individuals
who pursue their interests
without fencing each other in."

"This isn't a fence."
She pointed to her rib cage.

He saw her through shadows of
venetian blinds.

Massaging each other's fingers,
sometimes they'd dislocate.

STORAGE

The smoke goes out the smokestack
and then fades.
There are plenty of times you've complimented
my back. Your compliments are taken and walked
around with for months,
harbored in the spinal column,
which begins to love its place.

There are other things you’ve told me
about cameras and Kodachrome
that break into smoke
and fade.

There are whole households full of people
storing compliments in their bones.

OBSESSION

She was trying to tie a knot
with a stranger, assuming his features spoke
for themselves.

Assuming his love life with someone else
was nothing that beat into him
too strongly.

It would take her years to redefine the cushions
after he sat on them.

NOTHING LASTED LONG

There was so much Africa in his voice,
contemplation in his eyes,
and lust in his smock of wears,
But we were polka-dotted people
with our eyes closed.
Some said soul mates,
others said mating souls,
but nothing lasted long.
And the Jehovah's Witnesses were hiding in the bushes;
the Mickey Mouse night-light was dying down,
and all of China was tuckered out.

SHORT VISITS

Are you going to come and enjoy me for a few days
then echo off the buildings and bounce back home?
You know there are sharks with their undivided attention
waiting for me on the nearest corner.
There's pudding in the wastebasket and a reducible smile
in teeth.

FACING THE ATMOSPHERE

The atmosphere—face forward
in your business—

never promised more
than a flair
for throwing you.

Challenge was in the fans
batting the air around
like it was nobody's business.

We expect too much from those close to us,
as if they could fill the vastness
we push our expressions into.

At least she was unrefined,
able to create a gesture
without giving up
on its roots.

MISCALCULATIONS

They waited for the bus,
talking to each other as if they were best friends.
It was alarming the way
the sunlight hit them
in the eyes.

He didn't understand her detached retina
or that she was a product of her family's
miscalculations.

She and her family had had insecurities,
so they groomed each other
until they were finally willing to go outside.

Others actually liked them
and called them by their first names.
They scrunched this into their faces
but couldn't chew.

FRECKLED WITH CHANCE

The infancy of summer was devastated by his address.

Melodrama whacked into her system.

Purple flowers, the house of a man who never got fed

up with bachelorhood.

Misgivings in the pavement.

They were all freckled with chance in the boulevards.

A fragrance repeated in his mother's hair.

No one knew her better than her dependents.

The day was in the clutches of the laundromat.

The second half of our lives

THE SECOND HALF OF OUR LIVES

We are all friends who have lived our childhood
way into adulthood.

Childless, we go out for dinner.
There are no compromises.
Each limb is its own.

There's only the commotion of living
the second half of our lives
in the bulk of the first.

A SURVIVOR

The worst had happened.

Yet she woke up
every morning.

Her features still met the atmosphere
at the same coordinates.

THE PROCESSION

The hardships of tomorrow are put off
as we make our way to the grocery.

The living go to cafes
and discuss their injuries.

The dead keep their places
underfoot, marinating.

Meanwhile the procession of carts slows
in the paper towel aisle.

Those walking down the street with groceries
are indisputably of this time,
properly devoted to this century.

Tinfoil radiates off a windshield,
wrinkling the reflections of the passersby.

Humbling those who
are already humbled.

ORDER?

A bag slowly rolled down the housing project wall.
Things are constantly being lost
out of windows,
in the bathroom, down the hall.

I'm surprised people walk around intact.

But the reverse order of things springs at me
when I throw paper at the ground and it flies up.
Where the sky is dark, I think I'll be warm.
I can't stop thinking that the wrinkles in my toes
mean youth.

THIS AGE

By now you've seen quite a few days.
They've registered over your eyes
and can't explain themselves to the neighbors.

Aging is subtle
although now we can see it.
It's spelled out on our pillowcases.
The formalities are gone.

We have a better understanding of the weather
than our parents.
But our parents know best
how to live in it,
how to siphon it out of the pool.

MOM AND DAD GROWING OLD

She went back to her hometown.
The recesses between her parents'
teeth were growing wider,
but love still shined through the holes
in their knit sweaters
and kept things at a warm familiar pace
with lunch preceding dinner.

DECEMBERS IN MIAMI BEACH

Miami Beach was a place for my relatives' fit bodies
to lean back into the sun.
A place where they moved recklessly
out into the deep.

Years of the same backstroke,
the same straw hats,
and the sea
washing in and out
of their shades.

Then, one winter,
under the wide brims,
their trim middles
loosened.

Crumbly,
in the sand.

This was a matter discussed years ago
only now surfacing
in spots of light

on their faces
at midday.

GIVE OR TAKE

The water
made us forget the stretch of time that separated us,
pushed it under our feet with the rocks.
The waves
pushing us toward shore
                                        had the same effect on both of us
as nothing else had for the past year.
We dove under,
        ended up at parallel spots,
had to stand and press against the water to get back out.
The water pulled everything out of us
as it pushed us through
hair first.

We dove and laughed.

I mentioned the divers and cameras yards away,
probably looking for an old shipwreck.
Later, biking home,
we learned they had been looking for a woman.

The fisherman who found her the next morning
said at first he thought she was a mannequin
        lying across the rocks.

the
doing.

A MOMENT
IN SPANISH LAKES MOBILE HOME PARK

When Grandpa sleeps, all gravity falls
to his chin.
He is wearing his beige coat,
the one he's afraid of losing.
His shoulders fall as he exhales.
The fan above him flicks shadows
on and off his red- and white-striped pants.
Grandma is writing in her checkbook.
She sighs.
The park's clipped grass is dry, rough
and filled with lizards.
The canal is stagnant.
Watching TV, the Scottish couple next door
is heavy-hearted,
their son missing in Turkey.
The woman has four-inch toenails.

DAUGHTER UNDER WEEPING WILLOWS

It took months for the seed to meet the egg
and so many more for the formation
of the being,
who is now discussing the day with you,
"clear and cold," with bits of disturbing news
slipped under the fingernails.

Reclining in lawn chairs—
the impossibility
of what it means
to have created another,

who can talk shop with you,
the reflections of the trees swinging
in her hair.

And to think of others who had loved
and lost
this whole progression.

IN MEMORY OF ROSE ROSENBLATT

Grandma had a stout walk
and centuries of human nature
built up in her spine,
supporting her entrance into the restaurant.

Her sturdy body,
moving from bedroom
to kitchen,

always
had an opinion

recreated
in the lines
around my father's eyes.

MY DOG THAT DIED

They say my dog that died
looked like a seal.
I thought about my dog.
He didn't look like a seal to me.
But what is life anyway
that it can slide right under my dog and be gone?

It's experiencing a world,
a world where we can look at seals if we want to
or rhinoceroses or hippopotami if we want to.

And wherever we travel after this,
wherever this is leading,
will we be able to see these phenomena?
Or are seals only a one-life thing?

TOO FAR INTO PRODUCTION

The world was built up.

The origins of a century
that went too far into production
and skimped on the hand holding.

A paper towel after every washing.
A napkin for every cherry.

It didn't occur to them
to think of those who follow.

MY EX

He was too rigid
for children.

They would need
to rub up against his legs
like cats
and jump into his arms
without warning.

He needed his arms
to arm himself.

His kisses, brushes with promise,
twisted into the fetal position.

His crunch
is in my teeth
but my body is beginning to move on.

THERE WAS A PRICE TO BE PAID

There was a price to be paid
for having children

but a bigger price
for not

leading them from the park
to the playground
and showing them the ladybugs in your hair.

At the cafe, the boy left
his mother's table
to eat without her.

She resisted,
calling him over,

but he was struck
by the poster
of a fish in the Red Sea.

HOME

The backslap left an imprint of a hand
on her back

until someone took her in,
gave her a massage,

and they lived together
with their edges off,
no frills.

A number of things came back to her,
but the air, in particular,
accepted her more
on her own terms.

She had a home now—
a place to regurgitate
if she had to.